MW01679683

This journal belongs to:

Be Still My Soul

Be Still My Soul

A Devotional Journal for Boys

Jennifer Flanders

PRESCOTT PUBLISHING
Tyler, Texas

The vast majority of clip art in this book is from a set of 9 CDs my husband bought me back in 1996 called *Masterclips 101,000 Premium Images Collection*. This was long before I started blogging or writing or publishing *anything*, and I hadn't the foggiest idea what I'd ever do with such a thing — but I held onto it, just in case, and now I use it all the time!

 For information, please address Prescott Publishing, 3726 Woods Blvd, Tyler, TX 75707. http://prescottpublishing.org

ISBN: 978-1-938945-22-9
LCCN: 2014960030

Dedication

To my brave, brilliant,
Bible-believing sons,
with love

Contents

Introduction

This book belongs to you. There is no right or wrong way to complete it. You may use these pages to record thoughts, compose poetry, set goals, write prayers, paste photographs, paint pictures, draw sketches, make lists, tape mementos— or a combination of any or all of the above.

It is my hope that this little journal will get you thinking about the deeper things of life, such as who are you? Why are you here? And how can you live with meaning and purpose?

I believe the best place to find answers to such questions is through God's Word, so you'll find lots of Bible verses scattered throughout these pages.

Proverbs 23:7 tells us that as a person thinks in his heart, so is he. My goal in creating this little devotional journal is to get you thinking about God, about His great love for you, and about how you can live in a way that will bring glory and honor to Him.

The title of the book is taken from an old hymn I love, which you will find printed on the next page. Life is full of uncertainties, but we can be confident that the Lord is on our side, working everything together for our good and His glory. That knowledge should quiet, calm, and comfort our souls like nothing else.

May His richest blessings be yours,
Jennifer Flanders

Be Still, My Soul

by Catharina von Schlegel
translated by Jane Borthwick

Be still, my soul; the Lord is on thy side;
Bear patiently the cross of grief or pain;
Leave to thy God to order and provide;
In every change He faithful will remain.
Be still, my soul; thy best, thy heavenly, Friend
Through thorny ways leads to a joyful end.

Be still, my soul; thy God doth undertake
To guide the future as He has the past.
Thy hope, thy confidence, let nothing shake;
All now mysterious shall be bright at last.
Be still, my soul; the waves and winds still know
His voice who ruled them while He dwelt below.

Be still, my soul, though dearest friends depart
And all is darkened in the vale of tears;
Then shalt thou better know His love, His heart,
Who comes to soothe thy sorrows and thy fears.
Be still, my soul; thy Jesus can repay
From His own fulness all He takes away.

Be still, my soul; the hour is hastening on
When we shall be forever with the Lord,
When disappointment, grief, and fear are gone,
Sorrow forgot, love's purest joys restored.
Be still, my soul; when change and tears are past,
All safe and blessed we shall meet at last.

One time in my life when I could tell God was walking alongside me...

"The LORD is the one who goes ahead of you; He will be with you. He will not fail you or forsake you. Do not fear or be dismayed."

- Deuteronomy 31:8, NASB

This is how I know that I belong to God...

"If anyone acknowledges that Jesus is the Son of God,
God lives in them and they in God."

- 1 John 4:15, NIV

Childhood Memories

My Birth Statistics:

Name: ____

Birthdate: ____

Time: ____

Weight: ____

Length: ____

Location: ____

Parents: ____

____

"A woman giving birth to a child has pain because her time has come; but when her baby is born she forgets the anguish because of her joy that a child is born into the world."

- John 16:21, NIV

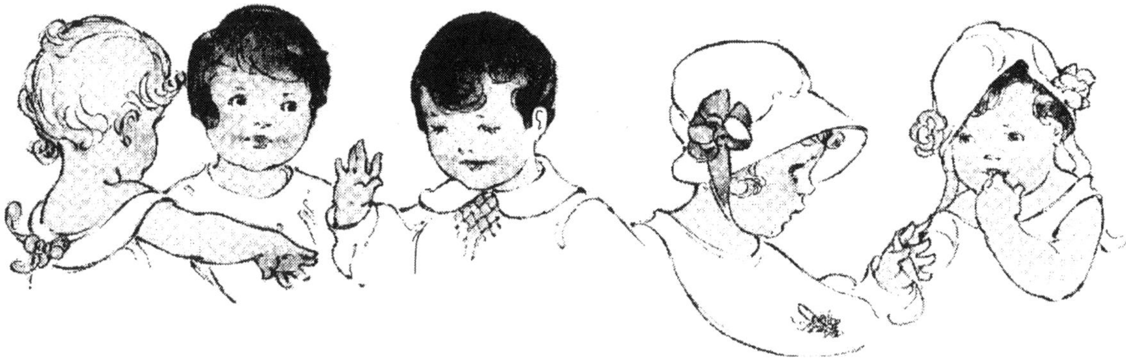

The meaning of my given name:

"A good name is to be more desired than great wealth,
Favor is better than silver and gold."

- Proverbs 22:1, NASB

My earliest memories from childhood...

"Brothers and sisters, don't think like children. When it comes to evil, be like babies, but think like mature people."

- 1 Corinthians 14:20, GWT

My childhood friends and playmates...

"A friend loves at all times, and a brother
is born for a time of adversity."

- Proverbs 17:17, NIV

... and the games we played

Books and stories I read and enjoyed as a child:

Books I want to read to my own children someday:

“One book, one pen, one child, and one teacher can change the world.

- Malala Yousafzai

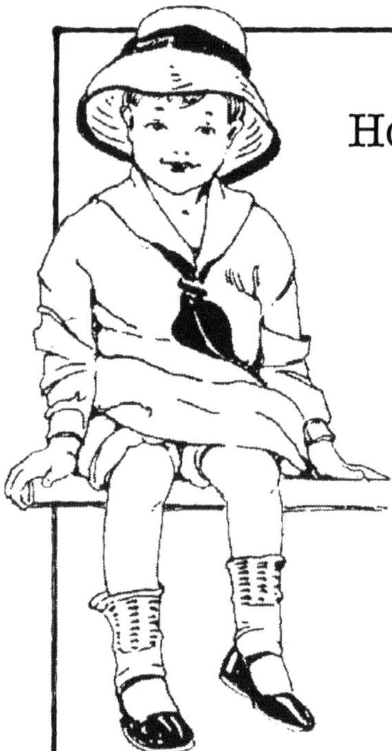

How I spent my days...

"A person's days are determined; You have decreed the number of his months and have set limits he cannot exceed."

- Job14:5, NIV

... when I was younger

God's view on children:

Luke 18:16

Psalm 127:3-5

Deuteronomy 7:13-14

Psalm 128:3-4

Behold,
Children are a gift
of the LORD.
The fruit of the womb
is a Reward.

- Psalm 127:3, NASB

Mistakes I have made...

"For all have sinned and fall short of the glory of God."

- Romans 3:23, NASB

... and lessons I have learned

Let no one look down on your youthfulness, but rather in speech, conduct, love, faith and purity, show yourself an example of those who believe.

- 1 Timothy 4:12, NASB

Special Christmas Memories:

"I will honor Christmas in my heart, and try to keep it all the year."

— Charles Dickens

Grade School Memories:

"The mind of the prudent acquires knowledge,
And the ear of the wise seeks knowledge."

- Proverbs 18:15, NASB

Summer Vacation Memories:

"As long as the earth endures, seedtime and harvest, cold and heat, summer and winter, day and night will never cease."

- Genesis 8:22, NIV

How Our Family Celebrates Birthdays

"Bring the fattened calf and kill it. Let's have a feast and celebrate."

- Luke 15:22-23, NIV

Special Birthday Memories

Childhood pets:

"The godly care for their animals,
but the wicked are always cruel."

- Proverbs 12:10, NLT

Memories of my first home:

"It will be a shelter and shade from the heat of the day, and a refuge and hiding place from the storm and rain."

- Isaiah 4:6, NIV

Be it ever so HUMBLE, There's No Place Like HOME.

- John Howard Payne

"When I was a child, I spoke and thought and reasoned as a child. But when I grew up, I put away childish things."

- 1 Corinthians 13:11, NLT

Wonderfully Made

"God created man in His own image, in the image of God He created him; male and female He created them."

Genesis 1:27, NASB

"My frame was not hidden from You, when I was made in secret,
And skillfully wrought in the depths of the earth...."

- Psalm 139:15

These are some things that make me unique:

"I praise you because I am fearfully and
wonderfully made; your works are wonderful,
I know that full well."

- Psalm 139:14, NIV

My eyes & how I see the world:

"Bright eyes encourage the heart; good news nourishes the body."

- Proverbs 15:30, ISV

My Hands

"Make it your ambition to lead a quiet life and
attend to your own business and work with your hands...."

- 1 Thessalonians 4:11, NASB

My Feet

"How beautiful… are the feet of the messenger who brings good news, the good news of peace and salvation, the news that the God of Israel reigns!"

- Isaiah 52:7, NIV

How can I best care for the body God has given me?

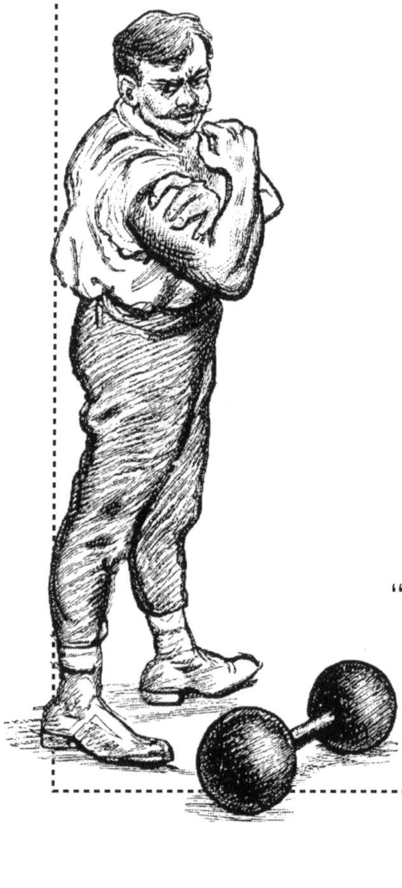

"Or do you not know that your body is a temple of the Holy Spirit who is in you, whom you have from God, and that you are not your own?"

- 1 Corinthians 6:19, NASB

"For You formed
my inward parts;
You wove me in my
mother's womb.
I will give thanks
to You, for I am
fearfully and
wonderfully made;
Wonderful are Your
works, and my soul
knows it very well." Psalm 139:13–14

God had a purpose for making me the way He did, and I should be thankful, even for the features I don't like.

"In every thing give thanks: for this is the will of God in Christ Jesus concerning you."

- 1 Thessalonians 5:18, KJV

"But who are you, a human being, to talk back to God? Shall what is formed say to the one who formed it, "Why did you make me like this?'"

- Roman 9:20, NIV

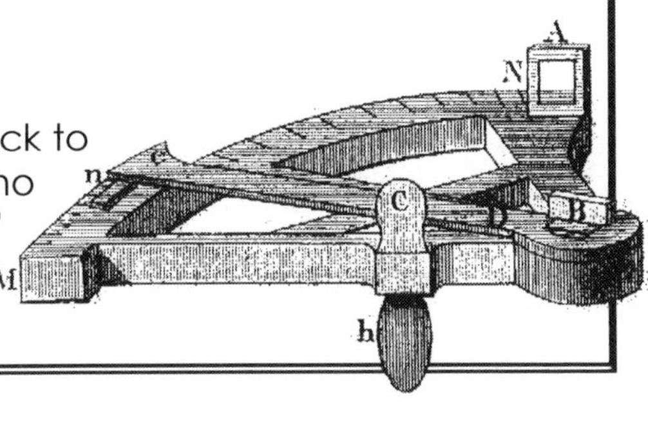

I need to make wise choices about what I eat...

"So whether you eat or drink or whatever you do, do it all for the glory of God."

- 1 Corinthians 10:31, NIV

... and I should also get plenty of exercise.

"Finally, my brethren,
be strong in the Lord, and in the
power of his might."

- Ephesians 6:10, KJV

"...while bodily training is of some value, godliness is of value in every way, as it holds promise for the present life and also for the life to come."

- 1 Timothy 4:8

Personal Favorites

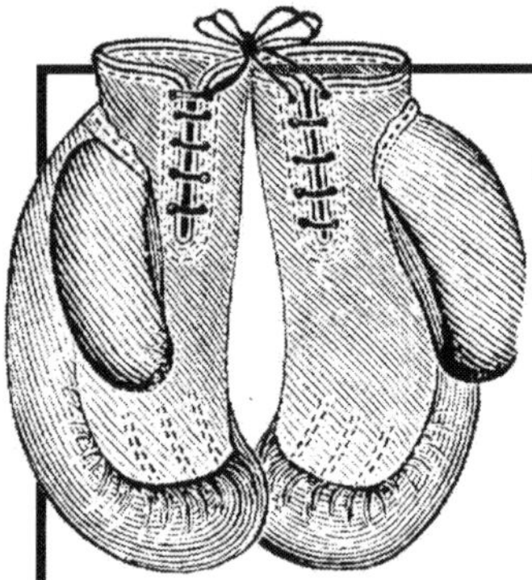

These are a few of my favorite things:

My Favorite Things

Rodgers and Hammerstein

Raindrops on roses and whiskers on kittens
Bright copper kettles and warm woolen mittens
Brown paper packages tied up with strings
These are a few of my favorite things

Cream colored ponies and crisp apple streudels
Doorbells and sleigh bells and schnitzel with noodles
Wild geese that fly with the moon on their wings
These are a few of my favorite things

Girls in white dresses with blue satin sashes
Snowflakes that stay on my nose and eyelashes
Silver white winters that melt into springs
These are a few of my favorite things

When the dog bites
When the bee stings
When I'm feeling sad
I simply remember my favorite things
And then I don't feel so bad

Favorite songs...

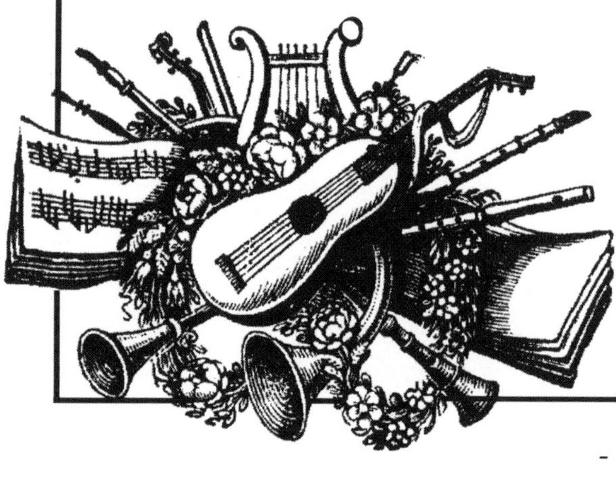

"Sing to the LORD a new song;
sing to the LORD, all the earth."

- Psalm 96:1, NASB

...and favorite verses

"Oh, how I love Your law!
I meditate on it all day long."

- Psalm 119:97, NIV

A Few More Favorites:

Favorite colors: ____________________________

____

Favorite foods: ____________________________

____

Favorite restaurants: ____________________________

____

Favorite animals: ____________________________

____

Favorite teachers: ____________________________

____

Favorite authors: ____________________________

____

Favorite musicians: ____________________________

____

Favorite movies: ____________________________

____

Favorite hobbies: ____________________________

____

My favorite school subject (and why):

"Study to show thyself approved unto God, a workman that needeth not to be ashamed, rightly dividing the word of truth."

- 2 Timothy 2:15, KJV

My closest friends...

"One who loves a pure heart and who speaks with grace will have the king for a friend."

- Proverbs 22:11, NIV

... and our favorite
things to do together

My normal bedtime routine...

"When I remember You on my bed,
I meditate on You in the night watches."

- Psalm 63:6, NASB

... and my favorite way to start a new day

"My voice shalt Thou hear in the morning, O LORD;
in the morning will I direct my prayer unto Thee, and will look up."

- Psalm 5:3, KJV

"Finally, brothers and sisters, whatever is true, whatever is noble, whatever is right, whatever is pure, whatever is lovely, whatever is admirable—if anything is excellent or praiseworthy—think about such things."

- Philippians 4:8, NIV

Thoughts to Ponder

"When times are good, be happy; but when times are bad, consider this: God has made the one as well as the other..."

- Ecclesiastes 7:14, NIV

"So teach us to number our days, That we may present to You a heart of wisdom."

- Psalm 90:12, NASB

Things I'm inclined to worry about...

"Search me, O God, and know my heart;
Try me and know my anxious thoughts."

- Psalm 139:23, NASB

What the Bible says about worry:

What I should do instead of worrying...

"Cast all your anxiety on Him because He cares for you."

- 1 Peter 5:7, NIV

Consider the lilies,
how they
grow: they neither
toil nor spin;
but I tell you,
not even Solomon
in all his glory
clothed himself
like one of these.

- Luke 12:27, NASB

God cares for me...

"Look at the birds of the air; they do not sow or reap or store away in barns, and yet your heavenly Father feeds them. Are you not much more valuable than they?"

- Matthew 6:26, NIV

... and He is the blessed controller of all things.

"Are not two sparrows sold for a cent? And yet not one of them will fall to the ground apart from your Father."

- Matthew 10:29, NASB

"When I consider Your heavens, the work of Your fingers,
the moon and the stars, which You have set in place...

... what is mankind that You are mindful of them,
human beings that You care for them?"

- Psalm 8:3-4

I must examine myself ...

"Examine yourselves to see whether you are in the faith; test yourselves. Do you not realize that Christ Jesus is in you—unless, of course, you fail the test?"

- 2 Corinthians 13:5, NIV

... and take every thought captive.

"We are destroying speculations and every lofty thing raised up against the knowledge of God, and we are taking every thought captive to the obedience of Christ."

- 2 Corinthians 10:5, NASB

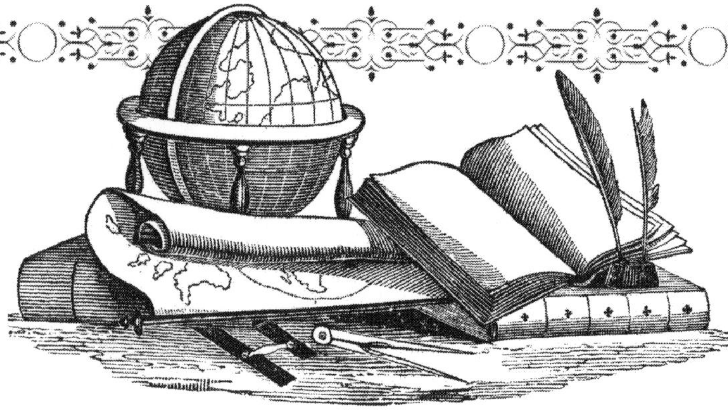

I should not imitate the world...

"And do not be conformed to this world, but be transformed by the renewing of your mind, so that you may prove what the will of God is, that which is good and acceptable and perfect."

- Romans 12:2, NASB

... instead, I should imitate God

(Ephesians 5:1)

"You are the light of the world. A city set on a hill cannot be hidden; nor does anyone light a lamp and put it under a basket, but on the lampstand, and it gives light to all who are in the house."

- Matthew 5:14-15, NASB

"'For My thoughts are not your thoughts, Nor are your ways My ways,' declares the LORD. 'For as the heavens are higher than the earth, So are My ways higher than your ways and My thoughts than your thoughts.'"

- Isaiah 55:9, NASB

The World Around Me

"In the beginning God created the heavens and the earth."

- Genesis 1:1, NIV

For the Earth is the LORD's and all it contains.

The heavens declare the glory of God...

... and the skies above
proclaim his handiwork.

- Psalm 19:1, ESV

Places I've been...

"But you will receive power when the Holy Spirit comes on you; and you will be my witnesses in Jerusalem, and in all Judea and Samaria, and to the ends of the earth."

- Acts 1:8, NASB

... and places I'd like to visit

"Go ye therefore, and teach all nations, baptizing them in the name of the Father, and of the Son, and of the Holy Ghost."

- Matthew 28:19, KJV

WHAT IN THE WORLD

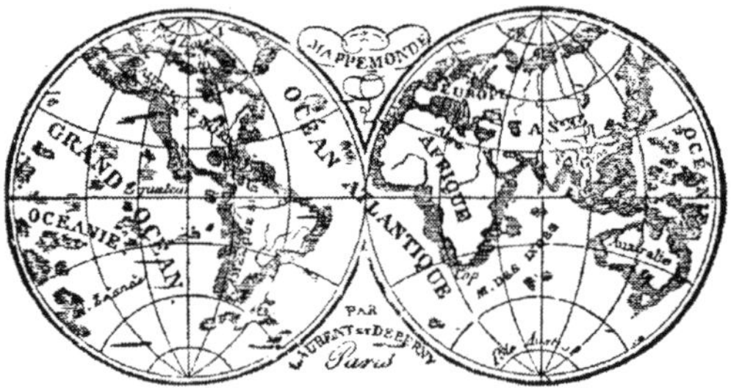

IS GOING ON HERE?

Current Events...

"When you hear of wars and rumors of wars, do not be alarmed.
Such things must happen, but the end is still to come.
Nation will rise against nation, and kingdom against kingdom.
There will be earthquakes in various places, and famines."

- Mark 13:7-8

... and what I think about them

How can I engage the culture?

"Defend the weak and
the fatherless; uphold the cause
of the poor and the oppressed."

- Psalm 82:3, NIV

... and reach the world for Christ?

"For God so loved the world, that He gave His only begotten Son, that whoever believes in Him shall not perish, but have eternal life."

- John 3:16, NASB

How can I conserve natural resources?

"Sluggards do not plow in season; so at harvest time they look but find nothing."

- Proverbs 20:4, NIV

... and be a good steward of the environment?

"Then the LORD God took
the man and put him into the garden
...to cultivate it and keep it."

- Genesis 2:15, NASB

"God has chosen the foolish things of the world to shame the wise, and God has chosen the weak things of the world to shame the things which are strong."

- 1 Corinthians 1:27, NASB

Prayers & Graces

It has been said that we should
"Pray hardest when it is hardest to pray."
During what times is it hardest for YOU to pray?

"But you, when you pray, go into your inner room, close your door and pray to your Father who is in secret, and your Father who sees what is done in secret will reward you."

- Matthew 6:6, NASB

PRAY WITHOUT CEASING

- 1 Thessalonians 5:17, NASB

"Be anxious for nothing, but in everything by prayer and supplication with thanksgiving let your requests be made known to God."

- Philippians 4:6, NASB

God's promises regarding prayer:

I should cultivate a constant attitude of prayer...

"Let us therefore come boldly unto the throne of grace, that we may obtain mercy, and find grace to help in time of need."

- Hebrews 4:16, KJV

My Parents Need Prayer

P is for Perspective

Pray that they would keep an eternal focus and would prioritize those things that God says are important. Ask God to give them wisdom and discernment in their dealings with you and with one another. (Psalm 90:12; Micah 6:8; James 1:5)

A is for Attitude

Ask God to give your parents a positive, cheerful outlook. Pray that the fruit of His Spirit would be evident in their lives, and that they would "do nothing from selfish ambition or vain conceit," but would instead model the "attitude that was also in Christ Jesus." (Proverbs 17:22; Galatians 5:22-23; Philippians 2:2-3)

R is for Relationships

Pray that God would bless and strengthen your parents' relationship to Him, to one another, and to their children and grandchildren. Pray their marriage would be characterized by an abiding, self-sacrificing love and a deep, heartfelt respect for one another. (Isaiah 41:10; Ephesians 5:33; Ephesians 6:1-4)

E is for Energy

Parenting is hard work! Pray that God would refresh and rejuvenate your mom and dad. Ask him to renew their strength and replenish their energy. Pray that they would not grow weary in well-doing, but would persevere to the end and finish strong. (Isaiah 40:28-31; Galatians 6:9-10; 2 Thessalonians 3:13)

N is for Needs

Ask God to provide for all your parents' needs "according to the riches of His glory in Christ Jesus." Pray that He would bless them abundantly, beyond all they ask or think, and that they would serve as an open channel of blessings to others. (Philippians 4:19; 2 Corinthians 9:18; Ephesians 3:20-21; Luke 6:38)

T is for Testimony

Pray that your parents would live their lives with integrity and that God would reward them with a good name. Pray that they would be salt and light in their community, and that the love of Christ would shine through them to a lost and dying world. (Proverbs 20:7; Proverbs 3:3-4; Matthew 5:13-14)

S is for Security

Pray that your parents would recognize God as the source of their security. Ask Him to do a work in their hearts, conforming them to the image of Christ and making sure their salvation. Pray that they would earnestly seek wisdom and would walk in their way securely. (Psalm 121; Psalm 127:1; Romans 12:2; Proverbs 3:23)

PRAISE

- Psalm 96:2 -

REPENT

- Acts 3:19 -

A

ASK

- 1 John 5:14 -

Y

YIELD

- Psalm 40:8 -

"You do not have, because you do not ask."

- James 4:2, NASB

"You ask and do not receive, because you ask with wrong motives, so that you may spend it on your pleasures."

- James 4:2, NASB

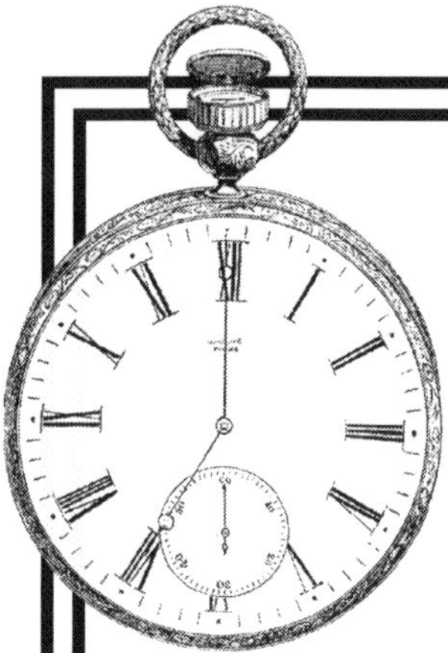

I should seek the LORD with my whole heart.

"Seek the LORD while He may be found; call on Him while he is near."

- Isaiah 55:6, NIV

ASK

and it shall be given unto you,

SEEK

and ye shall find,

KNOCK

and it shall be opened unto you.

- Luke 11:9, KJV -

"If you only pray when you're in trouble, you're in trouble."

(author unknown)

"Call upon Me in the day of trouble;
I shall rescue you, and you will honor Me."

- Psalm 50:15, NASB

My Requests & God's Answers

My prayers for myself:

"In the same way the Spirit also helps our weakness; for we do not know how to pray as we should, but the Spirit Himself intercedes for us with groanings too deep for words."

\- Romans 8:26, NASB

My prayers for my family:

My prayers for my friends:

"Dear friend, I pray that you may enjoy good health and that all may go well with you, even as your soul is getting along well."

- 3 John 1:2, NIV

My prayers for my church:

“As for other matters, brothers and sisters, pray for us that the message of the Lord may spread rapidly and be honored, just as it was with you.”

- 2 Thessalonians 3:1, NIV

My prayers for the sick:

"The prayer offered in faith will restore the one who is sick, and the Lord will raise him up, and if he has committed sins, they will be forgiven him."

- James 5:14, NASB

My prayers for the lost:

"For the Son of Man came to seek and to save the lost."

- Luke 19:10, NIV

My prayers for my leaders:

"I urge, then, first of all, that petitions, prayers, intercession and thanksgiving be made for all people—for kings and all those in authority, that we may live peaceful and quiet lives in all godliness and holiness."

- 1 Timothy 2:1-2, NIV

My prayers for my country:

"If My people, who are called by My name, will humble themselves and pray and seek My face and turn from their wicked ways, then I will hear from heaven, and I will forgive their sin and will heal their land."

- 2 Chronicles 7:14, NASB

Our Father

which art in heaven,
Hallowed be Thy name.
Thy kingdom come.
Thy will be done
in earth, as it is in heaven.
Give us this day our daily bread.
And forgive us our debts,
as we forgive our debtors.
And lead us not into temptation,
but deliver us from evil:
For Thine is the kingdom,
and the power, and the glory,
for ever. Amen.

- Matthew 6:9-13, NASB

Thy Will Be Done

"...nevertheless not my will, but Thine, be done."

- Luke 22:42, KJV

Therefore, confess your sins to one another,
and pray for one another so that you may be healed.
The effective prayer of a righteous man
can accomplish much."

- James 5:16, NASB

Family & Friends

"God sets the lonely in families..."

- Psalm 68:6

Family Record

Name	Relationship

I am thankful for my family:

"Enter into His gates with thanksgiving, and into His courts with praise: be thankful unto Him, and bless His name."

- Psalm 100:4, KJV

My Family Tree:

"And he shall be like a tree planted by the rivers of water, that bringeth forth his fruit in his season; his leaf also shall not wither; and whatsoever he doeth shall prosper."

- Psalm 1:3, KJV

I am thankful for my parents...

"Listen to your father, who gave you life, and do not despise your mother when she is old."

- Proverbs 23:22

What the Bible says about my relationship with my parents:

Children, obey your parents in the Lord, for this is right.

EPHESIANS 6:1

The kind of parent I want to be someday:

My siblings:

"Whoever claims to love God yet hates a brother or sister is a liar. For whoever does not love their brother and sister, whom they have seen, cannot love God, whom they have not seen."

- 1 John 4:20, NIV

How can I encourage them?

"Therefore encourage one another and build each other up,
just as in fact you are doing."

- 1 Thessalonians 5:11, NIV

My Friends:

"Do not forsake your friend or a friend of your family..."

- Proverbs 27:10, NIV

How can I be a better friend?

"As iron sharpens iron,
so a friend sharpens a friend."

- Proverbs 27:17, NLT

Qualities I admire in my old friends:

"Whoever walks with the wise becomes wise,
but the companion of fools will suffer harm."

\- Proverbs 13:20, ESV

Qualities I look for in new friends:

"The righteous choose their friends carefully, but the way of the wicked leads them astray."

- Proverbs 12:26, NIV

To have a friend,
I must be a friend:

"Let us consider how to stimulate one another to love and good deeds, not forsaking our own assembling together, as is the habit of some, but encouraging one another..." - Hebrews 10:24-25, NASB

Be kind to one another, tender-hearted, forgiving each other...

- Ephesians 4:32, NASB

"... Better is a neighbor who is near than a brother far away."
- Proverbs 27:10, NASB

Pastimes & Hobbies

"... live a life worthy of the Lord and please Him in every way: bearing fruit in every good work, growing in the knowledge of God."

- Colossians 1:10, NIV

Things I like to do for fun:

"And people should eat and drink and enjoy the fruits of their labor, for these are gifts from God."

- Ecclesiastes 3:13, NLT

Games and sports
I enjoy playing...

"Do you not know that those who run in a race all run, but only one receives the prize? Run in such a way that you may win."

- 1 Corinthians 9:24, NASB

... and others I'd like to learn

"Everyone who competes in the games exercises self-control in all things. They then do it to receive a perishable wreath, but we an imperishable...."

- 1 Corinthians 9:25, NASB

Musical instruments I can play:

"Sing to the LORD with grateful praise;
make music to our God on the harp."

- Psalm 147:7, NIV

... and instruments I'd like to play.

"Praise Him with trumpet sound;
Praise Him with harp and lyre.
Praise Him with timbrel and dancing;
Praise Him with stringed instruments
and pipe.
Praise Him with loud cymbals;
Praise Him with resounding cymbals."

- Psalm 150:3-5, NASB

MAKE A JOYFUL NOISE UNTO THE LORD ALL YE LANDS. SERVE THE LORD WITH GLADNESS, COME BEFORE HIS PRESENCE WITH SINGING.

PSALM 100:1-2

What the Bible says about music:

Creative arts I enjoy...

"...make it your ambition to lead a quiet life and attend to your own business and work with your hands.

- 1 Thessalonians 4:11, NASB

... and others I'd like to learn

"In all labor there is profit,
But mere talk leads only to
poverty."

- Proverbs 14:23, NASB

Here is a picture I drew myself:

"See with what large letters I am writing to you with my own hand."

- Galatians 6:11, NASB

... and here's a picture I painted.

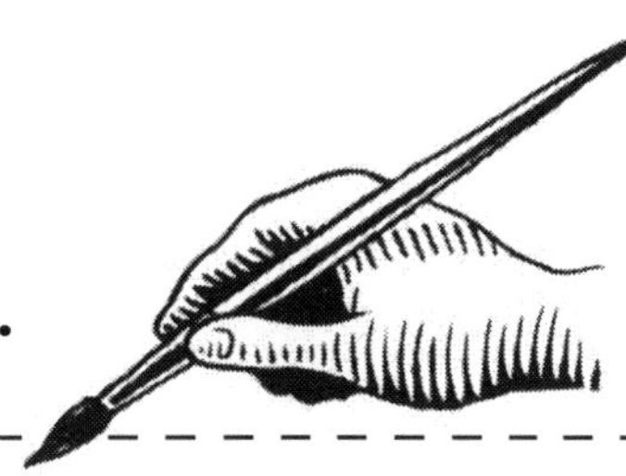

Activities I enjoy indoors...

"Look! I stand at the door and knock. If you hear My voice and open the door, I will come in, and we will share a meal together as friends."

- Revelation 3:20, NLT

... and out.

"Be wise in the way you act toward outsiders;
make the most of every opportunity."

- Colossians 4:5, NIV

Plants I've learned to identify...

"He makes grass grow for the cattle, and plants for people to cultivate—
bringing forth food from the earth:."

- Psalm 104:14, NIV

... and animals I've observed

"Do you know when the mountain goats give birth?
Do you watch when the doe bears her fawn?"

- Job 39:1, NIV

Special talents and skills that God has given me:

"To one he gave five talents, to another, two, and to another, one, each according to his own ability..."

- Matthew 25:15, NASB

How can I best use these gifts to glorify Him?

"Each of you should use whatever gift you have received to serve others, as faithful stewards of God's grace in its various forms."

- 1 Peter 4:10, NIV

"God is not unjust; He will not forget your work and the love you have shown Him as you have helped His people and continue to help them."

- Hebrews 6:10, NIV

A Heart for Service

"Whoever exalts himself shall be humbled;
and whoever humbles himself shall be exalted."

- Matthew 23:12, NASB

What the Bible says about serving others:

How can I serve my family?

"Whatever you do, do your work heartily,
as for the Lord rather than for men."

- Colossians 3:23, NASB

Different Chores that I Can Do

"Do everything without grumbling or arguing." - Philippians 2:14, NIV

Ages 2-3

- ☐ Put toys in toy box
- ☐ Stack books on shelf
- ☐ Place dirty clothes in laundry hamper
- ☐ Throw trash away
- ☐ Carry firewood
- ☐ Fold washcloths
- ☐ Set the table
- ☐ Fetch diapers & wipes
- ☐ Dust baseboards

Ages 4-5

- ☐ Feed pets
- ☐ Wipe up spills
- ☐ Put away toys
- ☐ Make the bed
- ☐ Straighten bedroom
- ☐ Water houseplants
- ☐ Sort clean silverware
- ☐ Prepare simple snacks
- ☐ Use hand-held vacuum
- ☐ Clear kitchen table
- ☐ Dry and put away dishes
- ☐ Disinfect doorknobs

Ages 6-7

- ☐ Gather trash
- ☐ Fold towels
- ☐ Dust mop floors
- ☐ Empty dishwasher
- ☐ Match clean socks
- ☐ Weed garden
- ☐ Rake leaves
- ☐ Peel potatoes or carrots
- ☐ Make salad
- ☐ Replace toilet paper roll

Ages 8-9

- ☐ Load dishwasher
- ☐ Change light bulbs
- ☐ Wash laundry
- ☐ Hang/fold clean clothes
- ☐ Dust furniture
- ☐ Spray off patio
- ☐ Put groceries away
- ☐ Scramble eggs
- ☐ Bake cookies
- ☐ Walk dogs
- ☐ Sweep porches
- ☐ Wipe off table

Ages 10-11

- ☐ Clean bathrooms
- ☐ Vacuum rugs
- ☐ Clean countertops
- ☐ Deep clean kitchen
- ☐ Prepare simple meal
- ☐ Mow lawn
- ☐ Bring in mail
- ☐ Do simple mending (hems, buttons, etc.)
- ☐ Sweep out garage

Ages 12 and up

- ☐ Mop floors
- ☐ Change overhead lights
- ☐ Wash/ vacuum car
- ☐ Trim hedges
- ☐ Paint walls
- ☐ Shop for groceries w/list
- ☐ Cook complete dinner
- ☐ Bake bread or cake
- ☐ Do simple home repairs
- ☐ Wash windows
- ☐ Iron clothes
- ☐ Watch younger siblings

I must train my eyes to look for ways to serve...

"Pure and undefiled religion in the sight of our God and Father is this:
to visit orphans and widows in their distress,
and to keep oneself unstained by the world."

- James 1:27, NASB

... and faithfully take advantage of the opportunities that present themselves.

"... serve one another humbly in love."

- Galatians 5:13, NIV

May God soften my heart ...

"Circumcise your heart,
and stiffen your neck no longer..."

- Deuteronomy 10:16, NASB

... to the plight of those in need

"Whoever oppresses the poor shows contempt for their Maker, but whoever is kind to the needy honors God."

- Proverbs 14:31, NIV

How might I help the needy?

"The generous will themselves be blessed,
for they share their food with the poor."

- Proverbs 22:9, NASB

What Scripture says about helping the poor:

Proverbs 19:7

Deut. 15:7-8

Proverbs 14:31

James 2:15-17

Proverbs 28:27

How can I live by the Golden Rule?

"Give, and it will be given to you.
A good measure, pressed down,
shaken together and running over,
will be poured into your lap.
For with the measure you use,
it will be measured to you."

- Luke 6:38, NIV

Do unto others as you would have them do unto you.

Luke 6:31, NIV

Whom do I know that is sick?

"Is anyone among you sick? Let them call the elders of the church to pray over them and anoint them with oil in the name of the Lord."

- James 5:14, NIV

What might I do to help or cheer them?

"Jesus went out, and he saw a great multitude.
He had compassion on them, and healed their sick."

- Matthew 14:14

A handwritten letter...

"I have no greater joy than to hear that my children are walking in the truth."

- 3 John 1:4, NIV

... would brighten anybody's day!

"Weeping may last through the night, but joy comes with the morning."

- Psalm 30:5, NLT

Just a few addresses for family and friends...

A
NAME: ______________________ ADDRESS: ______________________
CITY: ______________________ STATE: ________ ZIP: ______________

B
NAME: ______________________ ADDRESS: ______________________
CITY: ______________________ STATE: ________ ZIP: ______________

C
NAME: ______________________ ADDRESS: ______________________
CITY: ______________________ STATE: ________ ZIP: ______________

D
NAME: ______________________ ADDRESS: ______________________
CITY: ______________________ STATE: ________ ZIP: ______________

E
NAME: ______________________ ADDRESS: ______________________
CITY: ______________________ STATE: ________ ZIP: ______________

F
NAME: ______________________ ADDRESS: ______________________
CITY: ______________________ STATE: ________ ZIP: ______________

G
NAME: ______________________ ADDRESS: ______________________
CITY: ______________________ STATE: ________ ZIP: ______________

H
NAME: ______________________ ADDRESS: ______________________
CITY: ______________________ STATE: ________ ZIP: ______________

I
NAME: ______________________ ADDRESS: ______________________
CITY: ______________________ STATE: ________ ZIP: ______________

J
NAME: ______________________ ADDRESS: ______________________
CITY: ______________________ STATE: ________ ZIP: ______________

K
NAME: ______________________ ADDRESS: ______________________
CITY: ______________________ STATE: ________ ZIP: ______________

L
NAME: ______________________ ADDRESS: ______________________
CITY: ______________________ STATE: ________ ZIP: ______________

M
NAME: ______________________ ADDRESS: ______________________
CITY: ______________________ STATE: ________ ZIP: ______________

... who might enjoy getting a letter from me 

N NAME: ______________ ADDRESS: ______________
CITY: ______________ STATE: ______ ZIP: ______________

O NAME: ______________ ADDRESS: ______________
CITY: ______________ STATE: ______ ZIP: ______________

P NAME: ______________ ADDRESS: ______________
CITY: ______________ STATE: ______ ZIP: ______________

Q NAME: ______________ ADDRESS: ______________
CITY: ______________ STATE: ______ ZIP: ______________

R NAME: ______________ ADDRESS: ______________
CITY: ______________ STATE: ______ ZIP: ______________

S NAME: ______________ ADDRESS: ______________
CITY: ______________ STATE: ______ ZIP: ______________

T NAME: ______________ ADDRESS: ______________
CITY: ______________ STATE: ______ ZIP: ______________

U NAME: ______________ ADDRESS: ______________
CITY: ______________ STATE: ______ ZIP: ______________

V NAME: ______________ ADDRESS: ______________
CITY: ______________ STATE: ______ ZIP: ______________

W NAME: ______________ ADDRESS: ______________
CITY: ______________ STATE: ______ ZIP: ______________

X NAME: ______________ ADDRESS: ______________
CITY: ______________ STATE: ______ ZIP: ______________

Y NAME: ______________ ADDRESS: ______________
CITY: ______________ STATE: ______ ZIP: ______________

Z NAME: ______________ ADDRESS: ______________
CITY: ______________ STATE: ______ ZIP: ______________

Of course, phone calls are also nice!

"I have much more to say to you, but I don't want to write it with pen and ink."

- 3 John 1:13, NLT

A few important phone numbers:

name	number

"Call unto Me, and I will answer thee,
and show thee great and mighty things,
which thou knowest not."

- Jeremiah 33:3, KJV

"If you really keep the royal law found in Scripture,
'Love your neighbor as yourself,' you are doing right."
- James 2:8, NIV

Love Overflowing

"Now about your love for one another we do not need to write to you, for you yourselves have been taught by God to love each other."

- 1 Thessalonians 4:9, NIV

Our duty to our fellow man:

1 John 4:7

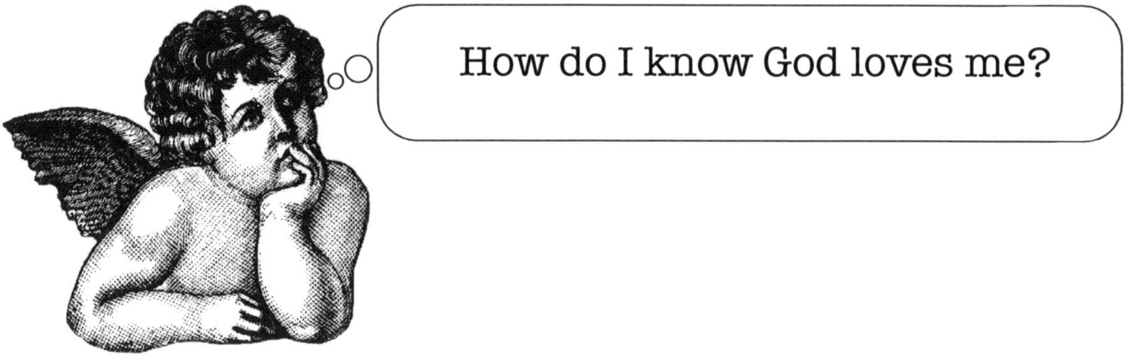

"But God demonstrates His own love toward us,
in that while we were yet sinners, Christ died for us."

- Romans 5:8, NASB

"For this is the love of God, that we keep His commandments; and His commandments are not burdensome."

\- 1 John 5:3, NASB

How do my family and friends know I love them?

"I thank my God upon every remembrance of you..."

- Philippians 1:3, KJV

How can I share God's love with others?

"A new command I give you: Love one another.
As I have loved you, so you must love one another."

- John 13:34, NASB

"Let love be without hypocrisy.
Abhor what is evil; cling to what is good."

- Romans 12:9, NASB

What the Bible says about love:

1 Corinthians
13 : 4-8

John
13 : 34

Matthew
5 : 43-45

1 Peter
3 : 8-9

Luke
6 32-35

Romans
13 : 8-9

1 John
4 : 20

LISTEN

"Whoever belongs to God
hears what God says."

- John 8:47, NIV

OBEY

"If you love Me,
obey My commandments."

- John 14:15, NLT

V

VALUE

"The LORD values the lives of His faithful followers."

- Psalm 116:15, NET

E

ENCOURAGE

"Encourage one another and build each other up."

-1 Thessalonians 5:17, NIV

LOVE is patient,
love is kind,
and is not jealous; love does not brag
and is not arrogant,
does not act unbecomingly;
it does not seek its own,
IS NOT PROVOKED,
does not take into account a wrong *suffered*,
does not rejoice in unrighteousness,
but rejoices with the truth;
bears all things,
believes all things,
hopes all things,
endures all things,
LOVE NEVER FAILS.

1 CORINTHIANS 13: 4 - 8

LET THIS BE YOUR GOAL

love
love
God is Love
- 1 John 4:8

"Greater love hath no man than this,
that a man lay down his life for his friends."

- John 15:13, KJV

Birthday Record

1
2
3
4
5
6
7
8
9
10
11
12
13
14
15
16
17
18
19
20
21
22
23
24
25
26
27
28
29
30
31

1
2
3
4
5
6
7
8
9
10
11
12
13
14
15
16
17
18
19
20
21
22
23
24
25
26
27
28
29

1
2
3
4
5
6
7
8
9
10
11
12
13
14
15
16
17
18
19
20
21
22
23
24
25
26
27
28
29
30
31

1
2
3
4
5
6
7
8
9
10
11
12
13
14
15
16
17
18
19
20
21
22
23
24
25
26
27
28
29
30

1
2
3
4
5
6
7
8
9
10
11
12
13
14
15
16
17
18
19
20
21
22
23
24
25
26
27
28
29
30
31

1
2
3
4
5
6
7
8
9
10
11
12
13
14
15
16
17
18
19
20
21
22
23
24
25
26
27
28
29
30

1
2
3
4
5
6
7
8
9
10
11
12
13
14
15
16
17
18
19
20
21
22
23
24
25
26
27
28
29
30
31

1
2
3
4
5
6
7
8
9
10
11
12
13
14
15
16
17
18
19
20
21
22
23
24
25
26
27
28
29
30
31

1
2
3
4
5
6
7
8
9
10
11
12
13
14
15
16
17
18
19
20
21
22
23
24
25
26
27
28
29
30

1
2
3
4
5
6
7
8
9
10
11
12
13
14
15
16
17
18
19
20
21
22
23
24
25
26
27
28
29
30
31

1 __________
2 __________
3 __________
4 __________
5 __________
6 __________
7 __________
8 __________
9 __________
10 __________
11 __________
12 __________
13 __________
14 __________
15 __________
16 __________
17 __________
18 __________
19 __________
20 __________
21 __________
22 __________
23 __________
24 __________
25 __________
26 __________
27 __________
28 __________
29 __________
30 __________

1 __________
2 __________
3 __________
4 __________
5 __________
6 __________
7 __________
8 __________
9 __________
10 __________
11 __________
12 __________
13 __________
14 __________
15 __________
16 __________
17 __________
18 __________
19 __________
20 __________
21 __________
22 __________
23 __________
24 __________
25 __________
26 __________
27 __________
28 __________
29 __________
30 __________
31 __________

One Last Word from the Author:

I hope you've enjoyed working your way through this book as much as I enjoyed creating it. Although I've been making and keeping personal journals and sketchbooks—and lots and lots of scrapbooks—for over forty years now, this is the first one I've ever designed for somebody else to use. I made it with my own boys in mind, but I thought perhaps other young men might like it, as well.

If that describes you, I would love for you to leave a positive review on Amazon, so other readers can get an idea of what the journal is like.

Additional volumes—including journals for teens, moms, and wives—will be released soon. If you have any questions or suggestions, feel free to contact me through my family's website, www.flandersfamily.info.

Although I read every message I receive, time constraits do not allow me to respond personally to most of them. Those twelve children you see standing beside me in the photo at the top of this page keep me far too busy for that, at least during this season of my life.

MORE GREAT BOOKS *for and about* LARGE FAMILIES

THE PRODIGY PROJECT is not your typical spy novel, but Jon Gunderson is not your typical spy. Devout Christian and devoted family man, join him as he hurries to China for his latest assignment, dragging his unsuspecting wife and their nine home schooled children along with him. The fate of the world hangs in the balance as the family take center stage against the backdrop of China's breathtaking landscapes.

As the father of twelve home schooled children, author Doug Flanders is well acquainted with non-stop adventure. He draws on fifteen years experience as an Army Reservist and twenty years as a practicing physician to craft his fast-paced, family-friendly novels.

GLAD TIDINGS

These refreshingly candid Christmas letters have been resonating with readers for 25 years. Now available for the first time in a single volume, together with collected quotes, favorite traditions, family recipes, and other assorted lists and ideas, Glad Tidings has something for everyone.

"I highly recommend this book. It shows the history of a family following God's will and call, and the blessings that followed!"

- Amazon reviewer M. McFarland

Available at Amazon, Barnes & Nobles and fine bookstores everywhere or order through Prescott Publishing at http:prescottpublishing.org

38916524R00118

Made in the USA
Charleston, SC
19 February 2015